A Guided Tour of
Apple Watch

Special Sales and Supply Queries

For any information about buying this title in bulk quantities, or for supply of this title for educational or fund-raising purposes, contact iTandCoffee on **1300 885 420** or email <u>enquiry@itandcoffee.com.au</u>.

iTandCoffee classes and private appointments

For queries about classes and private appointments with iTandCoffee, call **1300 885 420** or email **enquiry@itandcoffee.com.au**.

iTandCoffee operates in and around Camberwell, in Melbourne, Australia and offers remote support worldwide.

A Guided Tour of the
Apple Watch

TABLE OF CONTENTS

A Guided Tour of the
Apple Watch

TABLE OF CONTENTS

A Guided Tour of the
Apple Watch

TABLE OF CONTENTS

A Guided Tour of the
Apple Watch

TABLE OF CONTENTS

A Guided Tour of the
Apple Watch

TABLE OF CONTENTS

A Guided Tour of the Apple Watch

About this document

This book has been produced as a companion to the **Apple Watch Boot Camp** 3-part video class and series from iTandCoffee, so is designed to be used in conjunction with that series.

It has been produced using text and images from the class's slideshow, so the writing style for the majority of the book is 'bullet points' rather than detailed descriptions.

It is recommended that you refer to the corresponding videos if you need more detailed descriptions and discussions around each of the areas covered in this document.

Visit the **iTandCoffee** website – at www.itandcoffee.com.au/videos - for more information about how to access the **Apple Watch Boot Camp** video series – available in the iTandCoffee online Video Library to certain membership levels of the **iTandCoffee Club** (i.e. Online and Premium levels).

Learn more about the **iTandCoffee** Club, including its benefits and costs, at **www.itandcoffee.com.au/itandcoffee-club.**

In this guide (and the video series), we don't look at the variation in features between individual Watch models currently available and any earlier models, and we don't cover any buying recommendations for those purchasing their first Watch or looking to upgrade.

You can make a time with iTandCoffee if you need advice on this - or visit your local Apple retail store.

And there is no way we can cover every feature and app on the Watch in a guide like this. As for our iPhones, they are a bit of a 'bottomless pit' of features.

The aim of this guide (and the corresponding video series) is to provide a basis for you explore your Watch further, having established some basics and looked at some key features, settings and Apps.

A Guided Tour of the Apple Watch

Part 1

A Guided Tour of the Apple Watch
Part 1 – Getting Started

Introduction

Not all Apple Watches are made equal.

The functions that your Watch can perform will depend on when you purchased it and what type you purchased– ie. which Model you purchased.

To work out your Watch Model if you are not sure, visit https://support.apple.com/en-au/HT204507

Some Models have a built-in eSIM so they can be used 'on the go' (i.e. have internet/phone/ text access) without an iPhone being present. You pay a monthly fee to your Telco to use such an eSIM (eg. I pay Telstra $5/month)

Without an operational eSIM, you need an iPhone nearby for many functions of the Watch

It is highly recommended that you make sure you have a set of Bluetooth headphones to go with your Apple Watch, to allow you to listen to music and/or podcasts, talk on phone, give Siri instructions, and much more.

This frees you from having your iPhone on you all the time – on a walk or workout, doing the housework or some other activity where you don't necessarily have the iPhone in your hand or pocket.

Apple's Airpods work best, but other brands of Bluetooth headphones will also work.

A Guided Tour of the Apple Watch
Part 1 – Getting Started

In late 2022, the latest model Apple Watches are Watch 8, SE and Ultra. The 'from' prices for each of these models is shown below

New	New	New
Apple Watch Series 8	**Apple Watch SE**	**Apple Watch Ultra**
From A$629	From A$399	A$1,299

The Watch band you choose, and case material, will determine actual the price of the Watch.

Getting Set Up

The Watch App

- An Apple Watch must be associated with an iPhone for it to work
- Setup is from the **Watch** app on the iPhone
- From there, you choose what apps show on your Watch (more soon)
- You can also control how the Watch looks, settings and preferences, what music it holds, its apps, what it can do, and more
- Tap the **My Watch** option at the bottom left to view the settings for the Watch
- Well talk about the **Face Gallery** option shortly

Manage an Apple Watch for someone else

- An iPhone can have more than one Watch associated with it
- For example, a child's Watch (must be a Series 4 or later)
- The **Watch SE** model is a cheaper model of Watch, good for kids
- You add new watches from **All Watches** option at top left of the iPhone's **Watch** app

A Guided Tour of the Apple Watch
Part 1 – Getting Started

- Choose the **Add Watch** option
- You will then be asked if you wish to **Set Up for Myself** or **Set up for a Family Member**
- We won't go further into the process of setting up such a Watch, as the majority of readers of this guide will have Watch for just themselves.

Secure your Apple Watch

- Just like your iPhone, your Watch should have a Passcode – to keep it secure
- This Passcode only needs to be 4 Digits, but can be up to 10 digits – more secure
- Passcode can be set from Watch app or from the Watch itself
- We'll look at how to do this soon

A Guided Tour of the Apple Watch
Part 1 – Getting Started

Navigating – Buttons, Gestures, Areas

Digital Crown

- Press to see Apps
- Press again to get back to Watch face
- Rotate to scroll, adjust volume (depending on where you are)
- Double-press to return to previous app
- Long Press for Siri
- In some places, press takes you back a step
- When dimmed, press Digital Crown to 'wake up'
- Or rotate to gradually to turn on display (or wake by lifting your wrist)
- Various other functions when used in conjunction with Side Button (which we'll cover soon)

Side Button

- When the Watch is off, a long press of side button will turn it on
- Screen will be black at first, then Apple Symbol appears – it may be on the screen for a while before the watch face shows, so be patient
- If the Watch is fully off, you can press and hold the Digital Crown to quickly see the time – without having to power up the Watch
- One press from the clock or any app will give the **Dock** (which can be either Favourite apps or Recent apps – covered later)

A Guided Tour of the Apple Watch
Part 1 – Getting Started

- Double-press for **Apple Pay** (if Wallet is set up) – more on this later
- A very long press will call Emergency Services

 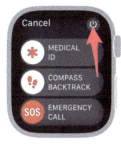 

- Long press also allows you to turn off – choose the symbol at top right and slide the dot across to confirm that you want to **Power Off**.
- Be careful not to keep holding the side button for too long, as it will make a call to Emergency Services if you do

How Often should I turn off?

- It is not necessary to turn off your Watch every day or regularly
- I rarely do this
- The only time I have done it lately is when I have had a glitch – for example, after a recent upgrade, the swipe up option would sometimes stop working
- Turning off and on fixed this

Combining Crown & Side Button

- Quick press of both together – **Screen Shot**
- Long press of both together – **Force Re-start** (if problem occurs)
- **To Force Quit an app**:
  - Press the Side Button until you see the power screen.
  - Then, press the Digital Crown until you return to the Watch face.

A Guided Tour of the Apple Watch
Part 1 – Getting Started

When should I Force Re-start?

- Force Restart is only required when your device is really misbehaving and where turning off and on doesn't help
- Hold both Digital Crown and Side button until screen goes black and let go only when Apple appears.

A Guided Tour of the Apple Watch
Part 1 – Getting Started

THE TAPS

Single Tap

- Tap the watch face to wake up your Watch (if you don't want to lift your wrist towards you)
- Tap a 'complication' on the watch face (if you have any) to open the app that it represents – more on 'complications' soon
- In various screens, tap to select or open

Force Touch (Long Press)

- A Force Touch is a long press and will reveal further options (if any are available) for the thing you force touched on.
- An example of where Force Touch applies is changing / editing Watch Faces (which we cover later)

The Swipes

- Swipe down from top: **Notification Centre**
- Swipe up from Bottom: **Control Centre**
- Swipe right to left: **Change Watch face** (if you have set up multiple)

What does the red dot at top mean?

- Do you see a red dot at the top of your Watch?
- This indicates there have been some Notifications
- Swipe down from to top to see these Notifications

Covering your Watch

- If your phone rings or is making a sound and you need to silence it quickly, just put your hand over the top of the watch face

A Guided Tour of the Apple Watch
Part 1 – Getting Started

Choose your Watch Face (or Faces)

Lots of options in the Watch app on iPhone

- The easiest way to set up your Watch is using the **Watch** app on the iPhone
- Certain settings/features can also be adjusted from the Watch itself, in the **Settings** app.
- Let's start with your Watch Face/s selection and customisation

First, Choose your Watch Face / Faces

- **My Faces** section at the top of the **Watch** app shows the faces that have been set up already
- New Faces can be added from the Watch itself or from the **Watch** App on iPhone
- In the Watch app, tap **Face Gallery** option (in bar along bottom)
- Scroll down to see a wide range of designs
- Tap to select any, and then view the options for customising the face

A Guided Tour of the Apple Watch
Part 1 – Getting Started

- Some faces have **Complications** – little symbols that provide quick access to an app, and sometimes also provide snippets of information

Customise your new Watch Face

- Customise the colour, style, dial symbols, etc of the chosen watch face (options/ customisations will differ across the watch faces)
- For example for Colour, tap each dot to see the effect (see previous page for images)
- Scroll down to adjust the **Complications** (see previous page for images)
- Tap each (for example, **Top Left**, **Top Right**, **Bottom Left**, **Bottom Right**) and choose the App that the Complication should represent
- Some watch faces have other Complication position descriptions in addition to (or

instead of) those mentioned above – such as **Sub-dial Left, Sub-dial Top**, etc.
- The example shown above right provides for up to 8 complications
- Others will provide less (perhaps none)

Add your new Watch Face

- Once you are happy with the watch face, tap **ADD**
- Your new Watch Face will then be added to the end of the list shown in **My Faces**
- The order of the Watch Faces on your Watch can then be adjusted

Manage Watch Faces

- Tap **My Watch** option (bottom left), then, tap **Edit** to see the list of Faces you have selected
- Tap 🔴 to delete any unwanted faces
- Touch and drag ▤ to re-order the faces
- Then tap **Done** (top right) when finished

Adjust your Watch Face

- Once the Watch Face is in **My Faces** list in the Watch app on the iPhone, tap it to adjust any of its settings
- From here, you can also **Set as current Watch Face** on your watch
- Or select the current watch face from the Watch itself

A Guided Tour of the Apple Watch
Part 1 – Getting Started

Adjust Watch Face from the Watch

- Each chosen Watch Face can be adjusted on the Watch itself
- **Force Touch** on the clock when it is visible on the screen
- You will see the screen change, with the **Edit** option at the bottom

- Swipe left-to-right (and v-v) to move through Watch Faces
- Tap **Edit** to customise the Face you are currently seeing
- As described above for the Watch app, different things about each Face can be changed

- Swipe left-to-right (and v-v) to move between the main customisation options that you see along the top.
- Some have STYLE, COLOUR and COMPLICATIONS
- For some, you also have BACKGROUND, DIAL COLOUR, etc as options

- Use the Digital Crown to change the STYLE of the Watch Face
- Then swipe left-to-right to get to the COLOUR options
- Rotate the Digital Crown to make Colour choice.
- And so on for the different options the Watch Face provides.

Choose your Watch Face's Complications

- Then choose/adjust the 'Complications' for the different parts of the Watch Face
- Tap each indicated area
- Then scroll up/down and tap to choose the app that should appear in that area
- For some apps, different options are provided for what information to show from that app

A Guided Tour of the Apple Watch
Part 1 – Getting Started

- Rotate crown or swipe up and down to view these options, then tap to select
- At any step, press the Digital Crown to go back a step
- Press multiple times to get back out of Edit mode

Using those Complications

- While some offer a snippet of information at a glance, other Complications simply provide quick access to an App or a particular part of an app
- Tap any Complication to view the App
- Then press the Digital Crown to return to the Watch Face

Adding a Watch Face from Watch

- Watch Faces can also be easily added from the Watch itself
- While viewing the clock, Force Touch on the screen
- Swipe from right to left until you see a screen with **New** at the top and a + in the middle
- Tap the +
- Scroll down to see watch face options and **Add** to add any faces you like

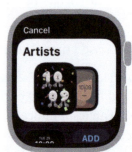

- Then follow steps described above to customise your selected Watch Face

A Guided Tour of the Apple Watch
Part 1 – Getting Started

One of my favourite Complications

- I have just added a Complication to my Watch that I am loving
- It allows me to quickly access my loyalty cards without needing my iPhone – simply by tapping the bottom left corner of my Watch to access the app **Stocard**
- When I tap a card name, it provides the barcode for scanning that loyalty card at the checkout (and the number, should there be any problem with scanning)
- I have found this much quicker that looking up the loyalty card in the Stocard app on my iPhone
- And I have really impressed shop assistants lately with this one!
- You must, of course, already have the Stocard app on your iPhone for this complication to be available.

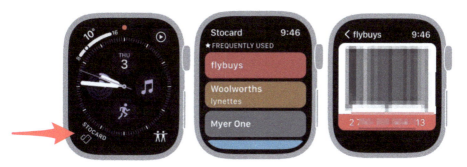

A Guided Tour of the Apple Watch
Part 1 – Getting Started

All those Apps

Viewing all those Apps

- To view all the apps that are on your Watch and select one, just press the Digital Crown
- Your apps may display in **Grid View**
- Rotate the Digital Crown to Zoom in and out in this view
- Tap to any App to open it
- Alternatively, your Apps can be displayed in **List View**
- I find this easier to use, as apps are listed alphabetically
- Rotate the Digital Crown or swipe the screen up and down to move through the list of apps
- Tap the required app to open it.

Choosing your App View

- From the Watch, open the **Settings** app
- Scroll down to **App View**
- Then tap the option you prefer
- Press the Digital Crown to return to your Watch Face
- The **App View** choice can also be made from the **Watch** app on your iPhone
- The change you make on iPhone will immediately appear on the Watch itself

A Guided Tour of the Apple Watch
Part 1 – Getting Started

Choosing what apps appear on the Watch

- The apps that you have on your iPhone may or may not have a Watch version of the app
- Any iPhone app that does have a Watch version can be added to the Watch (if it is not already on the Watch)
- This is done from **Watch** app on the iPhone – it can't be done from the Watch itself
- Scroll down to the section that is headed **INSTALLED ON APPLE WATCH** to see the non-standard apps that ARE already on the Watch

- Tap on any you don't want and turn off the **Show App on Apple Watch** setting to remove that app from the Watch
- Scroll down further to see the section headed **AVAILABLE APPS**, showing the Apps that do have a Watch version but that haven't yet been installed on the Watch.
- Tap **INSTALL** to add that app to the Watch
- The app will then appear in your App List (or in your Grid View) on your Watch
- Note that, for an app to be available to install on the Watch, it must already be downloaded to the iPhone.
- So if you are missing an app, see if you have perhaps removed it from your iPhone – and, if you have, go to the App Store and re-download it.

A Guided Tour of the Apple Watch

Part 2

A Guided Tour of the Apple Watch
Part 2 – Customising your Watch

Your Watch's 'Dock'

What is the Dock?

- On the iPhone/iPad, the Dock is the line of apps at the bottom of the Home Screen – which you generally set up to be your most frequently used apps
- While there is no line of apps at the bottom of the Watch screen, there is the Dock feature – accessible in a different way

Accessing the Dock

- You access the Watch's **Dock** using the Side Button
- A single press of the Side Button will show the Dock

What apps does the Dock show?

- The Dock can show EITHER the most recently used apps, OR your favourite apps (up to 10)
- This choice can be made from **Settings** on the Watch,
- It can also be made from iPhone's **Watch** app, from the **Dock** option there.

A Guided Tour of the Apple Watch
Part 2 – Customising your Watch

- I choose to show my **Favourites** apps in the **Dock**, instead of **Recent**s
- If you choose the **Favourites** option, ,setup of these Favourites must be done from the iPhone's **Watch** app

Choosing your Favourites for the Dock

- Go to the **Dock** option in the **Watch** app on the iPhone
- Choose **Edit** at top right to change the list of Favourites that appear here

- The Favourite apps are shown first, then the 'not included' apps.
- To remove an app from Favourites, tap
- To add to Favourites, tap
- Drag the right-hand lines   up or down to rearrange the list of Favourites
- Tap **Done** (top right) to finish

A Guided Tour of the Apple Watch
Part 2 – Customising your Watch

Some Important Settings

Set the text size (& other display settings)

- Is your Watch's text too small?
- Adjust this from iPhone's **Watch** app or from the Watch's **Settings** app
- In the iPhone's **Watch** app, go to **Display & Brightness** option
- Drag the **Text Size** slider to increase and decrease text size

- On the Watch, go to the **Settings** app, **Display & Brightness** option
- Tap the **Text Size** option
- Then tap the right-hand ᴀA to increase size, left ᴀA to decrease.

A Guided Tour of the Apple Watch
Part 2 – Customising your Watch

- Alternatively, turn the Digital Crown to adjust up and down
- Check out the other options here
- **Display and Brightness** option also allows brightness to be increased/ decreased – conserve the Watch's battery by lowering the brightness

- Choose **Bold Text** if needed
- For some models, scroll down to see the **Always On** option – turn On if you want the display to be always visible (just dimmed when you are not using it)

Waking up your Watch

- Various options are also available in **Display & Brightness** for **Wake** time and method for the Watch.
- Scroll down to see these options
- Turn off any that are not required
- Also select also how long the Watch should stay on when you wake it
- Longer Wake = higher battery usage

Standard replies to Messages

- It is worth setting up some standard replies to Messages, so that you can quickly respond from your Watch without having to type anything
- This setup must be done from **Watch** app on the iPhone
- Go to the **Messages** option (scroll down the main list to find this option in the list of apps provided in the **Watch** app)

A Guided Tour of the Apple Watch
Part 2 – Customising your Watch

- Tap the **Default** Replies option

- You will see a list of standard replies (which you can't change from here)

Tap **Add Reply** to add your own custom reply (and the rightmost image above shows an example of mine)

Your Watch as a bedside clock

- Your Watch can act as your bedside watch while it is charging overnight
- In both the iPhone **Watch** app and the Watch's **Settings** app, turn on **General -> Bedside Mode**

A Guided Tour of the Apple Watch
Part 2 – Customising your Watch

Control those Notifications

- Notifications will only appear on your Watch when you are not actively using your iPhone
- For your privacy, you can control how much and what Notifications are displayed when the Watch is locked, or when you are not looking at it
- And you can stop unwanted notifications
- Visit **Notification** in the Watch's **Settings** app or in the **Watch** app on iPhone
- For increased privacy, turn off **Show Summary When Locked**

- If this is left on, the name of sender shows when you receive a message, as in the example here – something you may not want if your watch is locked
- Choose to **Tap to Show Full Notification** to hide detail until you tap
- The List of Watch apps shows at bottom – tap each to control Notifications on a per app basis

A Guided Tour of the Apple Watch
Part 2 – Customising your Watch

- Different apps will have different options in terms of Notifications – options for Activity and Mail shown in the images on previous page

- For many (maybe most) apps, you will just choose **Mirror my iPhone** to allow the same notifications as on your iPhone.
- This is the default setting that will apply, but can be changed by exception
- There is also the **Show Notifications on Wrist Down** option in **Notifications**
- Turn off completely across all apps if desired
- Or, if on, turn off any apps that you don't want to provide notifications when your wrist is down.

- (Note. If you have already turned off Notifications for an App, you don't need to do the same here)

Return to Clock

- The **General** option (on both iPhone's Watch app and in the Watch's Settings app) has the **Return to Clock** option, which is above the **Bedside Mode** option
- This determines how quickly the clock re-appears after you launch an app
- Each app will have the **Default** setting initially, which is **After 2 minutes**

- Scroll down to see your list of apps and features and to set this individually for one or all of them (again, either from the Watch or iPhone)
- Tap **Custom** to set a non-standard delay for the selected app.
- Image on right shows the options that appear when you choose the **Custom** option – **Always**, **After 2 minutes** and **After 1 hour**

A Guided Tour of the Apple Watch
Part 2 – Customising your Watch

About your Watch

- It is worth checking out the other settings that are found in **General**
- **About** is where name of watch can be updated, version checked, Watch **Model** can be determined, serial number found, and more.

Software Update

- Visit **Software Update** to apply the latest update from Apple

A Guided Tour of the Apple Watch
Part 2 – Customising your Watch

If you are left-handed

- Change **Watch Orientation** if you want your Watch on the right wrist
- You can always choose which way the watch faces on your wrist – with the Digital crown on the left or right side.
- Left-handed people will usually want the **Digital Crown on Left Side** when the watch is on the right wrist

Your Watch's Storage

- As with any device, your Watch has a limited amount of storage available for apps and data
- Check the capacity and app data usages in the **Storage** option, available towards the end of the **General** set of options, on both the

A Guided Tour of the Apple Watch
Part 2 – Customising your Watch

iPhone **Watch** app and Watch's **Settings** app,

Aeroplane Mode Settings

- In the **General** option, establish if **Aeroplane Mode** should **Mirror iPhone**, or whether you want custom settings to apply when Aeroplane Mode is enabled

Secure your Apple Watch

- If you care about security, it is essential to turn on the Passcode feature of your Apple Watch
- The standard Watch Passcode length is 4 digits
- I choose a longer Passcode, because my Watch can **Apple Pay** without requiring any banking PIN (for purchases up to $200) – so I would not want the Watch passcode to be easily guessed if the Watch is stolen
- The Watch's passcode can only be numeric
- It can be the same as, or different to, the Passcode applicable to your iPhone.

A Guided Tour of the Apple Watch
Part 2 – Customising your Watch

- From the iPhone, go to **Watch** app's **Passcode** option
- Or, on Watch, go to **Settings -> Passcode**
- Turn off **Simple Passcode** to set a longer passcode.
- Enable **Unlock with iPhone** to avoid having to put in a Passcode to unlock the Watch if you have your iPhone with you
- **Erase Data** protects your Watch if someone unsuccessfully tries to guess your passcode 10 times (even if you that is you!)
- **Wrist Detection** ensures that the Watch locks when not on your wrist – also an essential security precaution.

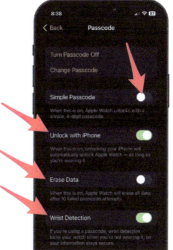

A look at Control Centre

What is Control Centre?

- Just as with iPhone, **Control Centre** is designed to give you quick access to various settings, features and apps
- Swipe up from bottom of the screen to access the **Control Centre**
- Drag upwards to see further options

Mobile Data

- First Control gives quick access to **Mobile Data** settings (only applicable if your Watch has an eSim).

Wi-Fi

- This Control allows you to quickly turn on/off **Wi-Fi** – or touch and hold to jump straight to the Wi-Fi settings

A Guided Tour of the Apple Watch
Part 2 – Customising your Watch

Ping iPhone

- If you have lost your iPhone, tap the third symbol (a vibrating iPhone) to 'ping' it so that you can locate it.

Battery

- Next control shows your battery % charge.
- Tap to go to **Battery** settings and, if you need to conserve, choose **Low Power Mode**

Mute

- Tap the bell symbol to **Mute** the ringer (red=muted)
- If it is already muted– tap to unmute

Theatre Mode

- The masks represent **Theatre Mode**
- Tap to enable – display will not show even if you lift your wrist, or for
notifications. Tap screen to turn on display.

Walkie Talkie

- Next symbol is the **Walkie Talkie**. For details of how to use this feature, see https://support.apple.com/en-au/HT208917

Focus

- The moon represents the **Focus** settings – tap to set a **Focus**
- If it is a colour, then one of your Focus types is turned on.
- Moon represents Do Not Disturb, but the symbol could be one of the others, as shown above - Work, Personal, Sleep or Driving
- We won't cover Focus in more detail here

Torch

- Next Control is the **Torch** – which shows a white backlit screen; wipe right to left to get a flashing light; again for a red light

A Guided Tour of the Apple Watch
Part 2 – Customising your Watch

- This would be useful at night in an emergency to flag down someone

Aeroplane Mode

- Then there is **Aeroplane Mode** – orange background when turned on. Make sure you use this when flying.

Water Lock

- The water drop turns on **Water Lock**
- Use Water Lock when swimming while wearing the Watch
- This locks the screen to stop water from causing unexpected things from happening (because screen is sensitive to the water touching it).
- Allows you to record activity (e.g swimming)
- Turn off this mode by pressing and holding the Digital Crown – which also ejects any water (you will feel a vibration)

Airplay

- Circles with upward arrow represents AirPlay
- On the Watch, it is how you chose which audio device to use with your Watch
- Tap to choose the device to which you would like to send the audio
- Once AirPods are connected, tap the same Control to see the options for using your AirPods with
  - Transparency
  - Noise Cancellation
  - Neither
- Try these out to see which works best

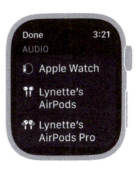

Headphone Volume

- 'Ear' symbol allows adjustment of headphone volume

A Guided Tour of the Apple Watch
Part 2 – Customising your Watch

Learning Mode

- The 'Person with hand raised' symbol allows the Watch to be placed into a mode called 'Learning' mode, where a simple clock is displayed, and other features are blocked
- Turn off by pressing and holding the Digital Crown

Text Size

- Quickly adjust the text size on your Watch, for apps that support something called Dynamic Type
- Use the Digital Crown to adjust the preferred text size (or tap AA at either end)
- Choose Done at top left when finished

Announce Notifications

- The bell symbol with lines on it allows you to turn on/off the **Announce Notifications** feature
- This feature is only available to tap when you are connected to AirPods (or some other audio device)
- Tap to enable (or disable) reading out of texts/notification that arrive while connected (red = enabled)
- Touch and hold it to see/select options

Choose your Controls

- The last option in the Control Centre is **Edit**
- Tap 🔴 to remove unwanted Controls
- Or 🟢 for addition of any missing Controls (listed at end under **MORE**)
- Touch and drag to rearrange order of Controls

A Guided Tour of the Apple Watch
Part 2 – Customising your Watch

- Make sure your most frequently used Controls are at the top, for easier access

A Guided Tour of the

Apple
Watch

Part 3

A Guided Tour of the Apple Watch
Part 3 – Day-to-Day Use

Use Siri – for lots of things

- If you enable Siri, you can talk to your Watch and ask Siri to call people, text, give directions, play music, and much more
- To ask Siri to do something, say **Hey Siri** – then speak your command

- OR long press on the Digital Crown – until you see the Siri 'orb' at the bottom of the screen (as shown on in the image on right), then give your instructions
- OR you can simply **Raise to Speak** – ie raise your watch towards you and then speak your command

- Set up these Siri options from iPhone **Watch** App's **Siri** option or from the same option in the Watch's **Settings** app.

Making and Receiving Calls

Answer your iPhone

- When your phone rings, your Watch will ring too (assuming you have default settings)
- If you can't find your iPhone, you can answer on your Watch and talk using your Watch
- Tap the green button to answer, or the red button to send the caller straight to Voicemail (if available)
- Another alternative is to tap the **...** for more options

- Scroll down to see a list of standard messages that you can send instead of answering the call
- You will also see the very handy option to **Answer on iPhone**
- If you choose this, the caller hears a 'Please Hold' message – giving you time to look for your iPhone
- The call shows as 'On Hold' on the Watch and on the iPhone (when you find it!)
- While you look for your iPhone, you can use your Watch to 'ping' your iPhone – using the symbol on left of the red dot

- Or you can just hang up using the red dot
- Or tap the **...** symbol at bottom right to see **Answer on Watch** or scroll down to **Send a Message**
- Note that the messages available under **Send a Message** are configured on your iPhone, from **Settings -> Phone -> Respond with Text**

If your Watch Doesn't Ring

- Open **Control Centre** and check for any of following
  - Ringer is red
  - Theatre Mode is orange
  - Focus has a colour (here showing Do Not Disturb)
- Tap to remove the colour from any of these – to turn them off - so that you will hear future notifications

A Guided Tour of the Apple Watch
Part 3 – Day-to-Day Use

Volume of ring/alerts is too low

- This is adjusted from the Watch's **Settings** app, from **Sounds & Haptics**
- It can also be modified from the **Watch** app on the iPhone, in the option by the same name

Call someone

- The easiest way to call someone is to use Siri
- Activate Siri using one of the methods listed earlier (*Hey Siri*, long press of Digital Crown, or raise your wrist before you speak)

- Then say '*Call John Smith*' (assuming John Smith is in your Contacts – as you can only ask to call or text people who are identified in your Contacts, and for whom you have recorded a phone number)
- If John Smith is in your Contacts with two phone numbers, you also have to say which one to use (e.g. 'Call John Smith Mobile')– or wait for Siri to ask you which one

A Guided Tour of the Apple Watch
Part 3 – Day-to-Day Use

- The long way to call someone is via the **Phone** app (which has the **Contacts** option)
- Set up your **Favourites** in iPhone's **Phone** app, for quick and easy access to your favourite Contacts from the Watch

- You can also call someone from the **Contacts** app
- Use the Digital Crown to scroll through Contacts (whether in Phone app or Contacts app) – faster turn causes letters to appear to help you find your Contact
- Tap the Contact, then tap the phone symbol to call
- Then tap either **FaceTime Audio** (if number is an Apple User's) or the phone number

Other options in **Phone** app are

- Dial a number using the **Keypad**

A Guided Tour of the Apple Watch
Part 3 – Day-to-Day Use

- Or check your **Voicemail** (more soon on this)

Returning Calls

- If you need to return a Recent call, go to the **Recent** option in the **Phone** app on the Watch
- Use **Digital Crown** to scroll up and down through **Recent** list – tap any entry to return that call

When you get a Voicemail

- If you miss a call, you will receive a notification about that missed call on your Watch (depending on your Notification settings and whether you have a Focus turned on)
- In the example below, I have swiped down from the top of the screen the see the Notification about the missed call, which went to my Voicemail
- If I tap on that Notification, it jumps me straight into my **Voicemail** option in the **Phone** app of the Watch

- I can then really quickly listen to my Voicemail via my Watch
- If I have my Air Pods in, I can then tap the green phone circle to return the call, or the bin to delete the Voicemail
- I have been using this a lot lately, instead of getting my iPhone out to listen to the Voicemail message.

A Guided Tour of the Apple Watch
Part 3 – Day-to-Day Use

Messages on your Watch

Receive and Read a Message

- Messages and other Notifications will only appear on your Watch when you are not actively using your iPhone
- They are also dependent on your **Notifications** settings (covered earlier)
- The images on the right shows the difference in the message preview if you have set the **Tap to Show Full Notification** turned on in **Notifications** settings (top image) or off (bottom image)
- Tap the Notification – which may be a banner at top of Watch screen – to view the message details & reply
- Scroll down for **Suggestions** (covered previously)

- Tap in the oval to type your message using watch keyboard
- OR tap the microphone on the keyboard to dictate
- OR choose to **Send Location** (under standard replies) so that someone else can find you easily.

A Guided Tour of the Apple Watch
Part 3 – Day-to-Day Use

Send a new Message

- As for calls, the easiest way is to talk to Siri – with **Hey Siri,** by pressing and holding the Digital Crown to activate Siri, or by raising your watch towards you and then speaking your command.
- *"Hey Siri,* text Jim Coulston I am running 5 minutes late"
- A preview of the message will show.
- Quicky tap **Don't Send** if there are any issues with what Siri 'heard'
- Otherwise, the message will send automatically in a couple of seconds

- The alternative is to go to **Messages app**

- Tap **New Message** to draft a new message
- Tap **Add Contact** to choose the recipient/s of the Message
- You will see a list of recently contacted people – choose one, or tap the middle symbol (see rightmost image above) to choose one from your list of Contacts (or use the microphone to 'speak' the person's name)
- Or tap the grid of dots to type the mobile number
- Tap **Create Message**
- Use one of the suggestions shown in the list at the bottom

- Or tap in the oval use the keyboard to use the keyboard to type your message – or the microphone to dictate it.

A Guided Tour of the Apple Watch
Part 3 – Day-to-Day Use

Music on your Watch

Play your favourite Music

- If you use Apple Music, or have purchased or sync'd music on your iPhone, you can play your music using the **Music** app on your Apple Watch
- You can also choose to store music on your Watch – so that it can play directly from there, rather than from the iPhone or via streaming
- If Music is not stored on your Watch, you must your carry the iPhone to play music – or have an eSIM in the Watch to stream it via the internet

Store Music on your Watch

- Selection of your Watch's stored music must be done from the iPhone's **Watch** app, via the **Music** option
- Choose whether **Recent Music** is added automatically to the Watch. In fact, this also enables downloads of recommendations from Apple Music – so you may get tracks you didn't expect (so turn this off if you don't want it).

A Guided Tour of the Apple Watch
Part 3 – Day-to-Day Use

- A list of the already-added Playlists and Albums shows at the bottom, under **PLAYLISTS & ALBUMS** heading
- Choose **Add Music** to add Playlists, Artists, Albums, from your iPhone's Music library.

 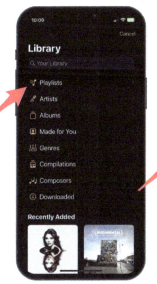 

- For example, above I tapped the Playlists option (shown in middle image above) to see my list of Playlists
- I then tapped on the Playlist I wanted to add
- I then tapped the ⊕ at top right to add that Playlist to the Watch.

A Guided Tour of the Apple Watch
Part 3 – Day-to-Day Use

Remove Stored Music

- Choose **Edit** at top right of the Music option (see last image on previous page) to manage the list of already-stored music
- Tap to remove any music that you no longer want on the Watch.
- Your Watch's storage capacity will limit how much music is able to be stored
- Check this in your Watch **Settings** (or iPhone's **Watch** app), in **General->Storage** (which we looked at earlier)

A quick look at the Music app

- Tap on the Music Complication on the Watch Face (that there is such a Complication on your Watch Face)
- Or select the Music app from your Watch's app list
- The currently playing song will usually show, allowing you to control the playback
  - arrow to start or re-start

  - vertical lines to pause

  - double-arrows to skip to next track or go back to previous

- When the 'now playing' screen is showing, turn the Digital Crown to turn music volume up and down

A Guided Tour of the Apple Watch
Part 3 – Day-to-Day Use

Option at bottom and top of Music app

- Bottom left symbol allows you to choose the output device (e.g Airpods) (see leftmost image below)
- Middle symbol allows you to see what's next and to shuffle, replay, etc (see middle image below)
- Rightmost symbol to add song to playlist, share and view other details (see rightmost image below)

- < at top left to see your Playlists and other options (keep tapping < to get back to 'top' level' of Music)
- When viewing top level of Music app (see second image below), scroll down to see albums and playlists, that you have chosen to store on the Watch

- Tap any album/playlist to select and start playing.
- Of course, there's lots more to the Music app that we haven't covered here. But hopefully there's enough in the above description to get you started.

A Guided Tour of the Apple Watch
Part 3 – Day-to-Day Use

Your Favourite Workout Music

- If you have a particular Music playlist that you like to listen to when 'working out' (e.g. on a walk or run), set this up in the **Watch** app on the iPhone, in the **Workout** option
- (This can't be set from the Watch – it must be done from the iPhone)
- Tap the **Workout Playlist** option

- You will see the list of Playlists that are available on your iPhone.
- Tap to select the Playlist you want for workouts.
- Also choose to **Play from Beginning** or **Shuffle** (see middle image above)

What if you use Spotify

- If you are a Spotify user, you can also play Spotify music from your Watch
- There is no problem controlling your Spotify music from your Watch if you have your iPhone with you.
- Just make sure that the Spotify app has been Installed on the Watch (see earlier in this guide for instructions on how to do this).

A Guided Tour of the Apple Watch
Part 3 – Day-to-Day Use

- If you want to download Spotify music to play without your iPhone, you must be a Premium subscriber
- And Watch must be at least a Series 3

Pay using your Apple Watch

- Your watch can be used to pay for things at the checkout
- If you don't have an eSIM in Watch, you must have your iPhone with you when your pay.
- Set up your payment methods for Apple Pay for your Watch in the **Watch** app on the iPhone, in the **Wallet & Apple Pay** option

- When you first set up **Apple Pay** for your Watch, you will see the list of credit cards that have already been set up on the iPhone, in **Settings -> Wallet & Apple Pay**
- Tap **Add** to add any of these as payment methods on your Watch
- **Add Card** to add another for your Watch only.
- Scroll down to choose your **Default Card** (see third image in the set above)
- To pay at the checkout, **double-press the side button**

A Guided Tour of the Apple Watch
Part 3 – Day-to-Day Use

- Then hold your Watch near the card reader to complete the transaction
- **If you have more than one card** …
- **Before** holding your Watch against the reader, choose which card to use by scrolling up/down to bring the required card into view
- Then hold your Watch near the card reader to pay with the selected card

Calculate something

- Your watch has a Calculator!
- Go to your App list and look for Calculator app
- Or (even better) you can ask Siri to do the calculation for you

Find Family People, Items, Devices

Find Devices

- We saw in the Control Centre (swipe up from bottom when positioned on clock) that you can quickly 'ping' your iPhone using a Control found there
- But you can also search for any devices associated with your Apple ID using your Watch, using the **Find Devices** app.
- Open **Find Devices**, then tap on any listed Device to see its location, set it to **Lost Mode, Play a Sound** – all functions that are available in the Find My app on the iPhone, iPad and Mac (and via iCloud.com)

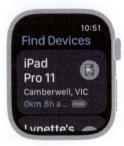

A Guided Tour of the Apple Watch
Part 3 – Day-to-Day Use

Find Items

- If you have AirTag/s (or other compatible 3rd party devices) associated with your Apple ID, locate them using your Watch's **Find Items** app
- These items must first have been associated with your Apple ID using the **Find My** app on iPhone, iPad or Mac.

Find People

- You can also locate your Family (those who have been set up in your iPhone's settings) – or anyone else who has shared their Location with you – using the Watch's **Find People** app
- Tap the person to see their location on a map, get directions, and set a Notification for when they leave

Check the Weather

- I use this one every day, multiple times
- Weather is an essential Complication to include on your Watch Face
- Tap the Complication to open Weather app (or go to Weather app)
- Tap to go between temp, forecast, and chance of rain by hour

A Guided Tour of the Apple Watch
Part 3 – Day-to-Day Use

- Scroll down to see more Weather info – UV Index, Wind Speed, Humidity, etc.
- App also shows forecast for next 10 days
- Current location is shown at the top left
- Tap `<` to see other locations and their current temp (and min/max), and tap any other location to see more details

A built-in Compass

- This handy App has been enhanced in **WatchOS 9**
- Work out your orientation
- Set a 'label' for your current location (bottom left symbol) – name defaults to date/time, adjust it to a better description
- Bottom right symbol is for 'Backtrack' – to re-trace your steps
- Tap symbol at top left to see further information about your current

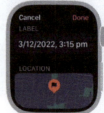

A Guided Tour of the Apple Watch
Part 3 – Day-to-Day Use

- This includes your altitude.
- The screen also shows your 'waypoints' – where car is parked, and other locations that you labelled

Podcasts

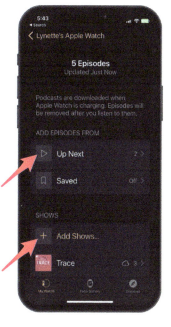

- If you are a Podcast fan, you can load Podcasts on to your Watch before you go out walking (similar to Music)
- Then you can listen to them without needing your iPhone or internet
- As with the Music app, you can view your library, the 'Listen Now' Podcast, and choose a Podcast that is on your iPhone but not on your Watch
- Podcasts in your 'Up Next' list are automatically downloaded while the Watch is charging and removed after you have listened –
- Tap **Up Next** to turn this Off.
- Choose **Add Shows** to add other Podcasts to your Watch

A Guided Tour of the Apple Watch
Part 3 – Day-to-Day Use

Your watch as a Camera Remote

- I love this feature!
- When you want to take a photo that includes yourself – perhaps as part of a group shot – you can set up your iPhone (or iPad) to 'point' at the photo subjects
- Then, you can jump into the shot and, from your Apple Watch, open the **Camera Remote** App
- Just wait a moment, and you will see what your camera is seeing
- When you are ready to take the shot, tap the **3s** 'dot' to take a photo
- Your watch will show a 3-second countdown and then take the photo from your iPhone

- If you don't want a countdown, tap the ... at bottom right before you take the photo, and turn off the **Timer** option (see leftmost image below)
- Scroll down for other options – which Camera to use (front or back), whether you want a Live photo, Flash, and HDR settings.

A Guided Tour of the Apple Watch
Part 3 – Day-to-Day Use

Help in an Emergency

Emergency SOS on your iPhone

- Emergency SOS is a feature of the iPhone
- It allows you to quickly contact emergency services in the case of an emergency – by applying a particular gesture (perhaps a choice of two)
- For iPhone, the feature settings are set up in **Settings -> Emergency SOS**
- Choose one or both of **Call with Hold** and **Call with 5 Presses**

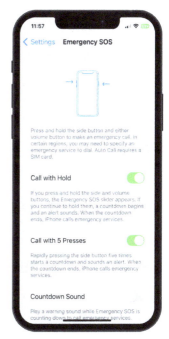

Emergency SOS on your Watch

- Your Watch also has Emergency SOS and can also call Emergency Services – manually or automatically
- Set this up from the **Watch** app on the iPhone
- OR go to **Settings -> SOS** on the Watch itself
- Turn on **Hold Side Button to Dial**
- This provides the capability to manually call emergency services
- To use, keep holding the side button until you see the services have been called.

Set up Fall Detection

- Your Watch can detect if you fall suddenly and don't seem to have moved
- Turn on **Fall Detection** to enable this feature

- This option is automatically enabled and set to **Always On** for anyone whose age is 50+
- If you don't get up after going down suddenly, your Watch will call Emergency Services on your behalf
- It will first alert you that a fall has been detected
- It will then sound an alarm giving you a chance to confirm you are OK
- If you do strenuous workouts, you may find the fall detection triggers when it shouldn't, and may find you need to turn it off.
- If you are younger and less concerned about falls, you can also choose to have this detection **Only on during workouts**

Set up Medical ID and more

- If there is no response when Emergency SOS is activated, Emergency Services will be called
- Your **Emergency Contacts** will also be notified – if they have been set up
- You set up your **Emergency Contacts** on the iPhone in **Settings -> Health -> Medical ID**
- Health Details and Medical ID can also be set up in the **Health** app on the iPhone
- Tap the 'account circle' at top right to find the **Medical ID** option
- Your **Medical ID and Emergency Contacts** are able to be accessed by

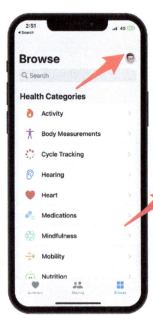
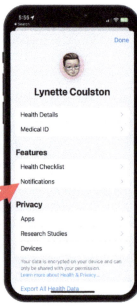

A Guided Tour of the Apple Watch
Part 3 – Day-to-Day Use

Emergency Services even if your iPhone or Watch are locked
- This means that, even if you are incapacitated and unable to unlock your iPhone or Watch, important information for your treatment/assistance can be easily accessed

Track your Activity

Activity App

- The **Activity** app shows your activity progress for the day, measured against your **Goals**, which are represented as 3 rings.
- You can set your **Goals** from within the **Activity** app on the Watch or from the **Fitness** app on the iPhone (we'll look at this shortly).
- Your Watch and iPhone measure your movement, exercise and stand progress for the day.
- 'Move' is represented as the pink outer ring, 'Exercise' is the middle green ring, and 'Stand' is the inner blue ring

- Scroll to the bottom see a **Weekly Summary**

A Guided Tour of the Apple Watch
Part 3 – Day-to-Day Use

- Or to **Change Goals**
- Choose **Next** to step through and review/adjust the Activity **Goals**.

View Activity in Fitness App on iPhone

- View more detailed activity stats and change goals from iPhone **Fitness** app (same symbol as the Activity app on the Watch)
- Here again, you tap the 'Account' circle at top right to establish basic details about yourself in **Health Details** (or go to **Settings -> Health** to do this)

- From here you can **Change Goals** to change your set of goals

A Guided Tour of the Apple Watch
Part 3 – Day-to-Day Use

Tracking your Workouts

- If you want to be sure your Walk (or run) distance/steps are recorded, make sure to start a Workout when you go on a walk.
- Because sometimes the auto-detection of a walk doesn't work kick in
- Best way is to add the **Workout** complication to your Watch Face
- In Workouts app, scroll down to choose the type of workout – then tap to select. 3-second countdown begins
- While you walk, you can view duration, heart BPM, distance, activity KJs, etc.

- Swipe upwards to view further details.
- To pause workout, swipe left to right and choose **Pause**
- Or press the Digital Crown and Side Button at same time.
- When done, swipe left to right in Workout app and choose **End**
- Summary of your workout shows – scroll to bottom and choose **Done**

Other Health Checks

Check your heart rate

- Your heart rate is automatically monitored when you are doing a Workout (see images on previous page)
- But you can check it any time from the **Heart Rate** app
- Scroll down to view your latest 'Resting Heart Rate', 'Walking Average', 'Outdoor Walk', and 'Post Workout' ranges/readings

Set Heart Rate Alert Levels

- Your Watch can monitor for low and high heart rate
- Set up notifications in relation to heart rate from **Settings -> Heart** on Watch or from **Watch** apps **Heart** option on iPhone
- In particular, set **High Heart Rate Notifications** for resting heart rate and **Low Heart Rate Notifications**
- Then choose what rate you deem to be low/high
- If your heart rate is above/below level for 10 mins you will get a notification on the Watch.

A Guided Tour of the Apple Watch
Part 3 – Day-to-Day Use

A built-in ECG (certain models only)

- Certain models of Watch can do an ECG
- Tap ECG app, then hold your finger on Digital Crown for 30 seconds while keeping your arm very still

- Obviously, this is not nearly as good as real thing - but it may help indicate if there is issue.

Check blood Oxygen level

- Tap the Blood Oxygen app then tap **Start**
- Your Watch must be snug on your wrist, and you must hold as still as you can, with your arm relaxed
- If you get **Unsuccessful Measurement**, choose **Dismiss** at bottom and try again

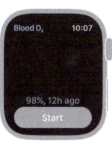

A Guided Tour of the Apple Watch
Part 3 – Day-to-Day Use

Sleep, Medications and Mindfulness

Monitor your Sleep

- Your Watch can monitor your sleep patterns and, if it is the newest Watch 8, can also record body temperature information as you sleep.
- In **Settings -> Sleep** on the Watch OR in the **Watch** app's **Sleep** option on the iPhone, set up whether the watch should track sleep and whether you should receive charging reminders before bedtime
- You then set up and manage your **Sleep Schedule** (and other settings) in the Sleep app on the Watch OR in the **Health** app on the iPhone, in the **Sleep** option (found when you choose **Browse**).
- You then need to wear your Watch as you sleep
- Your Watch display is locked during the scheduled sleep period, so that it doesn't wake you
- You will be woken with an alarm on your wrist at your defined 'wake' time

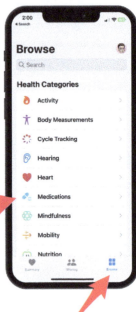

Manage your Medications

- Enter details of your **Medications** in the **Health** app on iPhone
- Tap the **Browse** option at bottom right to see this option in the list of categories.
- Select the **Medications** option

A Guided Tour of the Apple Watch
Part 3 – Day-to-Day Use

- Scroll down to the **Your Medications** section, choose **Add Medication** to add to your list of medications
- Choose **Edit** to change any details about the already-added medication
  (We won't go further into this aspect of the Health app in this guide.)

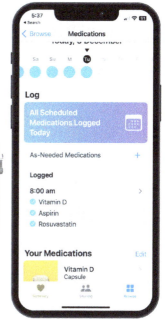

- Your **Watch** (and iPhone) will then provide reminder/s each day at a nominated time

- Tap **Log as Taken** when you get the reminder on your Watch (or iPhone)
- If you miss the reminder when it first comes in, go to your list of notifications (swipe down from the top of your Watch or iPhone) and tap on the medication reminder notification, and record **Log as Taken** (or otherwise)
- Or visit the **Medications** app on either the Watch or iPhone later to do this recording

Log your Medication Usage

- The **Medications** app on Watch shows whether any medications are due and allows you to record them as 'taken' or 'skipped'
- If you take multiple medications and all have been taken, scroll down and choose **Log All as Taken**

  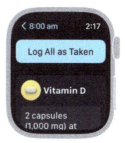

A Guided Tour of the Apple Watch
Part 3 – Day-to-Day Use

- Or scroll down to choose **Taken** or **Skipped** for each mediation

- You can also adjust the dose and time taken to change if needed - use digital crown to adjust each part of the time up & down

Take time for Mindfulness

- Your Watch can remind you to take time for **Mindfulness**
- Or you can choose at any time to do a Mindfulness exercise using your Watch.

A Guided Tour of the Apple Watch
Part 3 – Day-to-Day Use

- Set this up from the **Mindfulness** option of the **Watch** app on iPhone, OR from **Settings -> Mindfulness** on the Watch itself.
- (Note. There are additional options available in the **Watch** app on the iPhone to those found in settings on the Watch.)

Using Mindfulness

- There are 3 different mindfulness exercises -
    - Fitness+ Audio Meditations (part of the paid **Fitness+** paid subscription)
    - Reflect
    - Breath

Reflect exercise

- Below is an example of a **Reflect** exercise.
- Tap **Begin** to start, and you will see a lovely screen of moving colours/patterns – quite mesmerizing!
- To end at any point before the end of the mindfulness exercise, press the Digital Crown or swipe left and tap x

A Guided Tour of the Apple Watch
Part 3 – Day-to-Day Use

Breath exercise

- Breath in and out as instructed on the screen
- The exercise goes for 1 minute (tap ... to change this), and shows the results (eg heart rate) at the end

Another Very Quick look at the Health App

- You can see all the results and readings recorded by your Watch in the **Health** app on your iPhone
- **Summary** screen (bottom left option) gives latest stats, trends, readings, highlights, etc.
- Tap on any to view further details
- **Browse** option (at bottom right) gives full list of Health Categories
- Tap on each to see the latest and historical information that has been recorded by your Watch and your iPhone
- Tap any summaries you see there to view further break-down

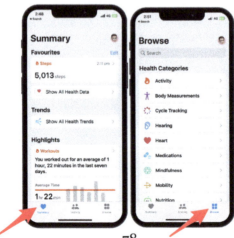

A Guided Tour of the Apple Watch
Part 3 – Day-to-Day Use

Fitness+

For anyone interested in making the most of their Apple Watch for fitness, Apple has the Fitness+ subscription, which provides all sorts of fitness routines that utilise the Apple Watch to record your workout during the routine.

You can watch a trainer take you through the exercise on your iPad or iPhone - or on a big screen using your Apple TV.

And, as described above, you also then get access to the Fitness+ Audio Meditations in the Mindfulness app.

New for the Watch 8 (new in 2022)

The latest Apple Watch, released in late 2022, included some great new features which we won't try to cover in this guide.

- Crash Detection – detects a sudden impact and like a car crash, and notifies emergency services
- A new built-in Skin Temperature Sensor
- Cycle Tracking using this temp sensor
  Sleep Tracking also uses temp sensor

Visit our Website

www.itandcoffee.com.au

Get personalised help with your technology

www.itandcoffee.com.au/help-with-technology

Join our iTandCoffee Club

www.itandcoffee.com.au/itandcoffee-club

Subscribe to our Newsletter

www.itandcoffee.com.au/newsletter

Check out what's on

www.itandcoffee.com.au/whats-on

View the range of iTandCoffee books

www.itandcoffee.com.au/guides

www.ingramcontent.com/pod-product-compliance
Lightning Source LLC
LaVergne TN
LVHW011803070326
832902LV00025B/4614